THE JOURNEY AND LIFE
THE UPSIDE OF AUTISM

Helping Jojo
with his daily skills.

Jojo differentiating his colours

Jojo explores different sports with his schoolmates.

Jojo is learning to skate with some classmates. Jojo is learning to ride a bike.

Jojo is learning to swim.

The chasing of Jojo in the neighborhood and the joy of him running into the neighbor's house.

Jojo goes to school giving high fives to everyone he sees.

Jojo goes shopping and runs through the aisles.

Jojo's unique love of food

Jojo's piano classes, the concert and the disappointment of losing his instructor.

Jojo's love and connection with family and neighbor and people, the joy of reaching out to others.

Jojo goes to the zoo and the moment at the bank.

BANK

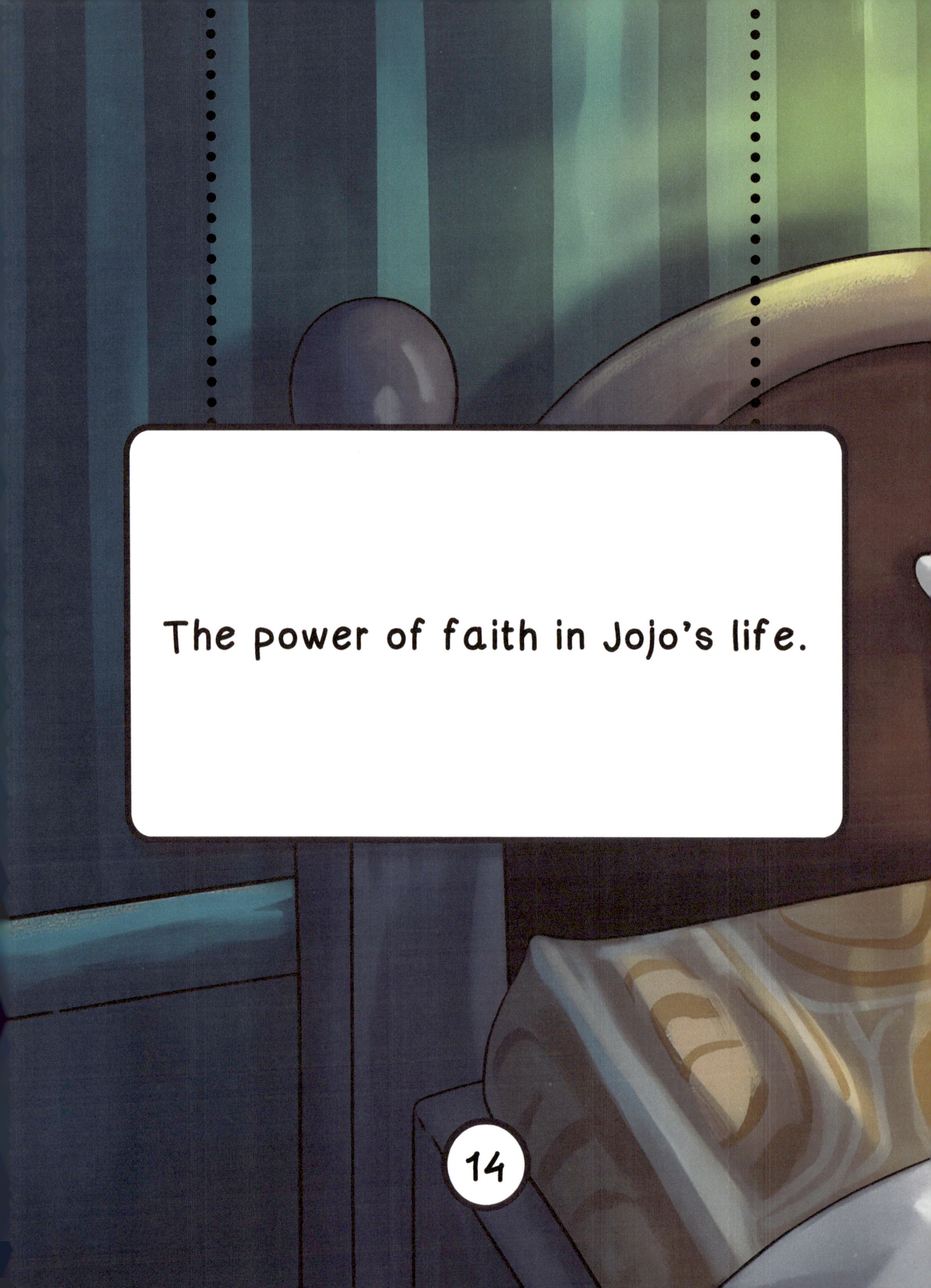

The power of faith in Jojo's life.

The challenges of autism. Everyone is special even with disabilities and God loves us all.

THE UPSIDE OF AUTISM

The Upside of Autism is a heartfelt journey through the triumphs and trials of raising a child with autism. Through intimate reflections and raw honesty, this book reveals the struggles, joys, and unexpected lessons learned along the way. Jojo's story is one of resilience, love, and the unbreakable bonds of family, showing how the most profound challenges can lead to the deepest growth.

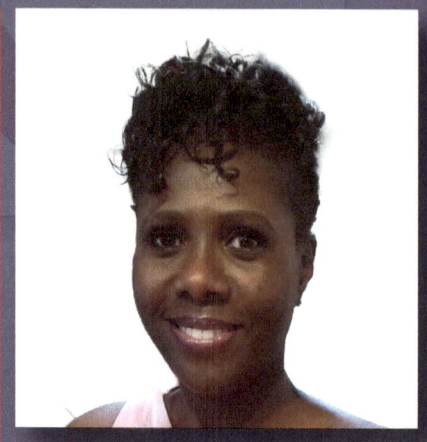

ESTHER CHRISTIANA SELLU

From his early days as a curious water baby to his love for sports, music, and food, Jojo's life is filled with moments of discovery and inspiration. Navigating school, social hurdles, and personal breakthroughs, his journey highlights the importance of patience, advocacy, and unwavering faith. With every challenge comes a revelation—one that reshapes the meaning of love and acceptance.

This book is not just about autism; it's about hope, transformation, and the power of belief. Whether you are a parent, educator, or someone seeking a deeper understanding of neurodiversity, The Upside of Autism gives a touching and enlightening perspective on embracing life's unexpected paths with an open heart.